· PERFECT PETS ·

Turtles

Susan Schafer

BENCHMARK BOOKS

MARSHALL CAVENDISH

NEW YORK

Benchmark Books
Marshall Cavendish Corporation
99 White Plains Road
Tarrytown, New York 10591

Library of Congress Cataloging-in-Publication Data
Schafer, Susan.
Turtles / Susan Schafer.
p.   cm. — (Perfect pets)
Includes bibliographical references (p.   ).
Summary: Describes the characteristics, habits, habitat, and history of the turtle and how to raise it as a pet.
ISBN 0-7614-0796-0 (lib. bdg.)
1. Turtles—Juvenile literature. [1. Turtles.] I. Title. II. Series.
QL666.C5S225   1999   597.92—DC21   97-40464   CIP   AC

Photo research by Ellen and Matthew Dudley

Cover photo: *Photo Researchers:* Leonard Lee Rue III
Back cover photo: *Reneé Stockdale*

The photographs in this book are used by permission and through the courtesy of: *Animals Animals:* Bill Beatty, 3; Robert Winslow, 6; Carsen Baldwin, Jr., 16; Breck P. Kent, 18 (top), 24; C. W. Schwartz, 18 (bottom); Zig Leszczynski, 21; Joe McDonald, 27; Joe & Carol McDonald, 29. *Art Resource:* The Pierpont Morgan Library/Art Resource, NY, 7; Foto Marburg/Art Resource, NY, 8. *Norvia Behling:* 23, 28. *Photo Researchers:* Francois Gohier, title page; Frans Lanting, 4, 19; Suen-O Linblad, 10; Andrew G. Wood, 12 (top); Jeffrey W. Lang, 12 (bottom); Joseph T. Collins, 14; Renee Lynn, 30. *Reneé Stockdale:* 20 (top and bottom), 22, 26. *Susan Schafer:* 13, 15.

Printed in Hong Kong
6   5   4   3   2   1

*To My Sweet Cheyenne
and to the protectors
of turtles everywhere*

*With special thanks to Dennis Sheridan
and to Paul*

A giant tortoise rests on top of a volcano in the Galapagos Islands.

Turtles

Slow and steady wins the race. The hare learned that lesson when it ran a race against the turtle in Aesop's famous tale. The hare was so sure it could run faster than the turtle that it decided to take a nap along the way. But the hare slept too long, and the turtle, at a slow and steady pace, crossed the finish line first.

People have been telling fables like Aesop's hare and the turtle for more than two thousand years. Depending on the country and the animals found there, the story changes. Instead of a hare, the runner might be an ostrich, an antelope, or a deer. The turtle, however, always wins the race.

In reality, the hare is faster than the turtle. If you were a jockey riding the fastest horse in the biggest race of the year, the hare could pass you by. The land turtle, or **tortoise**, with its heavy shell and stumpy legs, might take an hour to travel two city blocks.

A rabbit and a turtle. Which would win if they really ran a race?

On the other hand, if you put the hare in the ocean, the sea turtle would streak by it like a speedboat. The sea turtle can swim in the ocean almost as fast as the hare can run on land.

Turtles on land are slow, but all turtles can live for a long time. Some, such as the giant tortoises, live well over a hundred years. Many people think that the older you get, the

The stories of Aesop were told in Greece as long ago as 450 B.C. Each story has a moral or lesson to be learned. Against the slow and steady turtle, the hare learns that bragging won't win a race.

wiser you become. So in many parts of the world, such as China and India, turtles are not only symbols of steadiness and patience, but also of health, wisdom, and long life. For this reason, they are often believed to bring good luck.

The Turtle Who Holds Up The World

Many people long ago believed that a great turtle held the world on the shell of its back. Early North American natives thought the turtle was the only animal strong enough to keep the world stable. They also believed that earthquakes occurred when the turtle moved. According to Hindu priests in India, four sacred elephants stood on the turtle's back and helped support the world.

Aldabra tortoises feasting on leaves. Leaves from nonpoisonous plants like the mulberry and hibiscus make a nutritious addition to any pet tortoise's diet.

More

than 200 million years ago, the ancestors of modern turtles swam with the dinosaurs. When the dinosaurs disappeared, the turtles survived. Today more than two hundred and forty different **species**, or special kinds, of turtles live on Earth. These reptiles have changed so little since the time of the dinosaurs that they are sometimes called **living fossils**.

Because of its shell, everyone knows what a turtle looks like. The shell, like a suit of armor, helps protect the turtle from its enemies. Made of bone, it is heavy and rigid, so a turtle cannot run, jump, hop, or fly. Imagine how hard it would be to jog if you were carrying a bathtub on your back.

Turtles that live in water have lighter shells than those that live on land because they need to swim. Their shells are flatter and thinner. Instead of stout legs and feet for walking, they have flippers for paddling.

Turtles live on every continent except Antarctica, but most are found in the tropics. They live in forests, jungles, grasslands, deserts, and bodies of water. Some are smaller than a potato, while others are longer than a king-size bed.

Sea turtles live their entire lives in the ocean, sometimes traveling very long distances in search of food or mates.

They are grouped into families based on the kinds of bones they have in their skulls and shells. The pig-nosed turtles, soft-shelled turtles, river turtles, snapping turtles, and big-headed turtles are found in rivers, streams, lakes, and ponds. Tortoises live only on land. Freshwater turtles, mud turtles, and side-necked turtles live both on land and in fresh water. Sea turtles live only in the ocean.

When swimming underwater, the pig-nosed turtle can use its long nose like a snorkel.

A Shell With Rings

A turtle's outer shell is made up of sections called **scutes,** which fit together like the pieces of a puzzle. As the shell grows, rings form around the edges of the scutes. You cannot tell a turtle's age, however, by counting the rings, because more than one ring is added each year. In order to determine its age, you must know when the turtle hatched from its egg. Instead of a birthday, it has a "hatchday."

Turtles have been kept as pets for hundreds of years, but they are not **domesticated** like cats and dogs. They are still wild animals. They have been collected as pets and hunted for their shells and meat, and because of this many are now endangered. That means they are disappearing from Earth.

For that reason, never take a turtle out of its **habitat** or buy one that comes from the wild. Many towns and cities have turtle and tortoise clubs whose members breed and raise turtles in **captivity** and rescue abandoned turtles. They can help you choose the right turtle and tell you how to take care of it. Turtles bred in captivity live longer as pets

The snapping turtle eats any animal it can catch in its strong jaws.

than those taken from the wild. Abandoned turtles also need good homes.

While turtles are popular as pets, they are also a big responsibility. Because they live so long, deciding to keep one can be a lifetime commitment. In fact, your own children or grandchildren may have to take care of your pet turtle someday.

The Oldest Turtle

Turtles like this giant Galapagos tortoise live longer than any other land animal. The age record is held by another giant, a Seychelles tortoise, that lived at a military base on an island off Africa for 152 years. Since it was already fully grown when it was captured, it might have been more than 200 years old!

Turtles are not only popular today, but they were probably among the first wild animals ever to be kept as pets.

Turtles

are not for those who want a pet to cuddle. Holding them can upset them and make them sick. They are fun to watch, however, and they are smart. Some learn to recognize their owners, following them when they are hungry. Others respond to the sound of their owners' voices.

Many turtles, however, pull their heads into their shells when approached. Not many animals carry a place to hide right on their own back. Land turtles also hide in holes, and water turtles may dive into the water. They are not being intentionally rude. Remember, they are wild animals, and their **instincts** tell them to hide when larger animals come near. If they didn't protect themselves, they would not live long in the wild.

Turtles use their sharp eyes to spot **predators** and also to find food. Depending on where they live, they may eat plants, insects, or small animals. Because many turtles eat fruit, they are attracted to red and yellow colors. Pet turtles need to be protected from eating something they shouldn't, such as a red plastic toy or a bit of yellow cloth.

When frightened, a box turtle can pull in its head, legs, and tail and hide inside its shell.

Before a turtle eats something, it usually smells it first. If it likes what it smells, it opens its birdlike beak and bites off a chunk. That might include your finger, so be careful! Turtles don't have teeth, but their beaks are as sharp as garden shears. They have good hearing, although they often do not react to sound. For this reason, some people think they are deaf.

Aquatic turtles, such as pond turtles and mud turtles, make good pets. So do box turtles and tortoises, such as the gopher tortoise and spurred tortoise.

Once a pet turtle gets used to its new home, it may not hide as often.

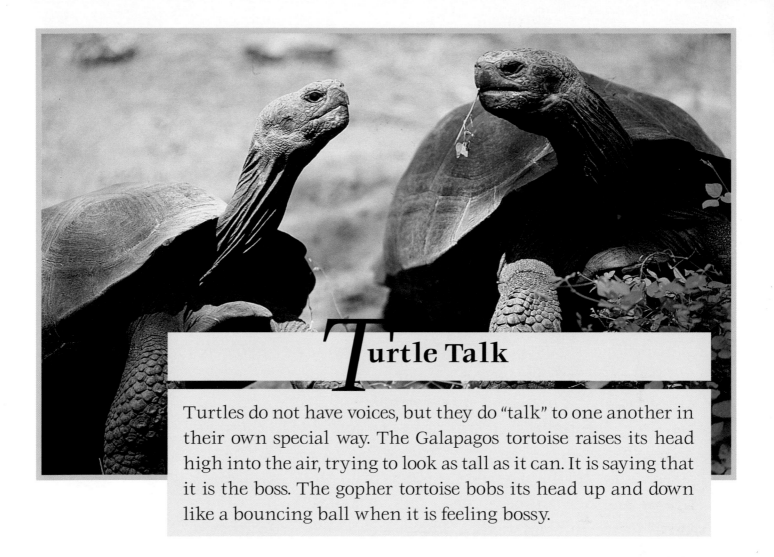

Turtle Talk

Turtles do not have voices, but they do "talk" to one another in their own special way. The Galapagos tortoise raises its head high into the air, trying to look as tall as it can. It is saying that it is the boss. The gopher tortoise bobs its head up and down like a bouncing ball when it is feeling bossy.

Many turtles, however, are protected by law, so make sure you get one legally through a turtle and tortoise club. Find out as much as you can about your turtle and what it needs *before* you bring it home. Then you can have everything ready for it.

Turtles need two roomy cages: one outside when the weather is warm and one inside during the winter or when the weather is cold. Each cage should have one warm side in

A turtle's cage should be simply furnished because everything will have to be taken out and cleaned regularly.

the sun or heated with a lamp and one cool side in the shade or away from the heat.

Because turtles are reptiles, they need the sun or another source of heat, such as a heat lamp, to warm their bodies. Their dark shells absorb heat. Once they are warm, their shells act like blankets when the day cools down.

If a turtle gets too hot, it will need to move to a cool or shady place; otherwise, it will over-heat and die. By moving in and out of the sun and shade, it will keep its temperature just right. For strong shells and bones, turtles need

Stacked rocks may collapse and crush a turtle. It is better to build or buy a small house where it can hide.

at least an hour of natural sunlight every day—or whenever the weather permits.

At night or when the weather is cold, turtles in the wild dive to the bottom of a pond or crawl into a hole in the ground. Water turtles that are kept outside as pets need a pond at least as deep as a meter- or yardstick. You can use a natural pond or build one yourself. The sides of the pond should slope gently so the turtles can easily crawl out of the water.

Land turtles need a house to crawl into. The house should be well insulated, dry, and free from drafts of cold air. You can build one yourself out of wood.

Box turtles and tortoises do not need ponds, but they do

The pancake tortoise is the flattest turtle in the world.

need a shallow pool or pan to sit in or drink from. To protect them from drowning, their water should never be higher than the bottom part of their shells.

Some turtles may need to hibernate for two or three months during the winter. This happens because their bodies slow down when temperatures drop. They stop eating, burrow underground, and "sleep" until spring. Hibernating a pet can be tricky, however, so for the safety of your turtle, ask someone with experience at a turtle and tortoise club to help you.

The bottom of a turtle's cage may be covered with potting soil, peat moss, or alfalfa pellets used for rabbits. Never use

Turtle Tips

Pet turtles need to be protected. They should not be able to climb out of their cages or dig under rocks that might crush them. Dogs, cats, and wild animals such as foxes and raccoons should not be able to get to them. To hold a turtle, always grasp it firmly with both hands. If it is dropped, its shell might break.

sand, gravel, ground corn cobs, perlite, cat-box litter, or wood-shavings, because your turtle can get sick if it eats some. Cleanliness is essential. A turtle's cage, pond, food dish, and drinking water must always be kept fresh and clean.

A box turtle enjoys a sunny day outside.

This box turtle with yellow-brown eyes is a female. Males have red-orange eyes.

Like

people, turtles need a balanced diet that includes many kinds of foods. Unlike people, however, they do not need to eat three meals a day. Feed them once a day, even though they may not always eat. Many reptiles can skip meals and still be healthy. Always offer them a little more food than they can finish.

Tortoises eat vegetables, such as collards, kale, turnip and dandelion greens, hibiscus, broccoli, alfalfa sprouts, shredded carrots, brussels sprouts, string beans, and grass. Do not feed them spinach, rhubarb leaves, beets, or cauliflower, because these are poisonous to turtles.

Mix some chopped fruit with the vegetables each day. Try apples, tomatoes, grapes, peaches, pears, plums, figs, papayas, mangoes, strawberries, or blackberries. If your turtle is a picky eater, mix its favorite food with its other food so it will have to eat everything to get what it likes.

Mud turtles and pond turtles are mainly meat eaters. Offer them earthworms, aquatic worms from a tropical fish store, fresh beef heart, and fresh, whole fish, such as guppies, goldfish, or sardines. Do not feed turtles frozen, thawed fish

Offering food on a flat, unbreakable pan or plate keeps it clean and makes it easier for a turtle to reach.

because it does not have the vitamins that they need for good health. And *never* feed them any kind of dog or cat food.

Mud and pond turtles also eat insects—such as crickets, waxworms, mealworms, silkworms, tomato worms, and grasshoppers—along with some fruits and vegetables. Put insects in the refrigerator before you feed your pet so the insects will move slowly enough for your turtle to catch.

The box turtle—so named because it can completely close itself up inside its shell as if it were a box—eats vegetables, fruits, meats, and insects. Most turtles eat late in the morning, after they have had time to warm up. If they are too cold, they cannot digest their food.

Keep plants out of the reach of turtles! Because a turtle may try to taste any plant in your house or yard, make sure none of them are poisonous to your pet

Like any other pet, a sick turtle may need to be checked by a veterinarian.

For strong shells and bones, turtles need vitamins added to their food. Fill a salt shaker halfway with powdered calcium carbonate, which you can find at a pharmacy, and the rest of the way with a powdered vitamin made especially for reptiles. Mix well and sprinkle over your turtle's food every time you feed it. Before feeding insects to your pet, coat them with a little powder. You can do this by shaking the insects and powder together in a plastic jar or paper sack.

To keep track of your pet's health, weigh it regularly. If it stays the same weight or gains weight, it is probably healthy. If it loses a lot of weight or has a bubbly nose, weepy eyes, or gurgling breath, it needs to see a **veterinarian** who treats reptiles. To protect your own health, *always* wash your hands with an antibacterial soap immediately after you handle a turtle.

If you decide you no longer want your turtle, you must

find someone to adopt it. Never let it go into the wild. It would not know how to survive, and it might give a disease to a healthy, wild turtle. Better yet, never get a turtle unless you are absolutely sure that you want to take care of it for the rest of its life. Only then will you be rewarded with years of fascinating fun and entertainment as you watch your unique, leathery-skinned friend flourish and grow.

A boy relaxing with his pet turtle.

Fun Facts

A group of Asian four-toed tortoises were the first animals more advanced than an insect to orbit the moon. They flew aboard the U.S.S.R. Zond 5 probe in 1968.

The leatherback sea turtle is the world's largest turtle. It can weigh as much as two horses put together!

The speckled tortoise of Africa is the world's smallest turtle. As an adult, it weighs about the same as an apple.

The African pancake tortoise is the flattest turtle. Its body is as flat as a short stack of pancakes, so it can squeeze into cracks under rocks.

To the ancient people of South America, the group of stars called Orion, the Hunter, was a mother turtle with her eggs who rose to the sky after a great flood.

The spurred tortoise from the island of Madagascar, off the coast of Africa, is the world's rarest turtle. Fewer than twenty survive in the wild.

A single sea turtle can lay up to a thousand eggs during one nest-building season—more than enough to fill eighty-three egg cartons and an entire refrigerator.

Glossary

captivity: The condition of being caught and held in a confined area.

domesticate: To tame an animal.

habitat: The area or kind of environment in which an animal normally lives.

instincts: Ways of behaving that are natural to animals from the time they are born or hatched.

living fossil: A plant or animal that looks the same today as its ancestors did in prehistoric times.

predator: An animal that lives by killing and eating other animals.

scutes: Thin, horny plates that cover the outside of a turtle's bony shell.

species: A group of animals that are descended from the same ancestor and are alike in certain ways.

tortoise: A special kind of turtle that lives on land.

veterinarian: A doctor who takes care of animals.

Find Out More About Turtles

Call the reptile department at a local zoo and ask for the name of the turtle club nearest you, or check out the list of reptile societies at *www.sonic.net/~melissk/society.html#societies* on the World Wide Web.

Coborn, John. *Turtles Today: a Complete and Up-to-date Guide.* Philadelphia: Chelsea House Publishers, 1997.

Fine, Edith Hope. *The Turtle and Tortoise.* Mankato, MN: Crestwood House, 1988.

Obst, Fritz Jurgen. *Turtles, Tortoises and Terrapins.* New York: St. Martin's Press, 1986.

Schafer, Susan. *The Galapagos Tortoise.* New York: Dillon Press, Macmillan Publishing Company, 1992.

About the Author

Susan Schafer's affection for turtles began while she was studying giant tortoises on the Galapagos Islands, and it continued to grow over seventeen years while she worked at the San Diego Zoo. She has written books for children about the Galapagos tortoise, the Komodo dragon, and the vulture. She lives on a ranch outside San Luis Obispo, California, with her husband, two horses, two dogs, and the native turtles that live in the ponds around her home.